What I Meant to Say Was…

By

Gary D. Grossman

Cover designed by Gary D. Grossman

ISBN: 978-1-915819-43-7

For: Barbara, Rachel and Anna, who have given me the gift of hope and contentment, as well as the freedom to write our truth.

OTHER TITLES BY IMPSPIRED

Maybury –
by Mary Farrell

The Metaphysics of Now -
by Jim Bates

Rattlesnakes and Flattops –
by Mackenzie Thorn

Leviathan -
by Jae Jenkins Scott

Irish Hares & Seahorses –
by North Coast Writers

Classical Adaptations –
by Susie Gharib

The River –
by Theresa C. Gaynord

Acknowledgements

I appreciate the constructive comments on the ms. by: Scott Ferry, Kim Malinowski, Robbi Nestor, and Arthur Stewart. These poems in various forms represent works written over the last two years and published or appearing in:

Blue Heron Review — Blessings,
Defenestration – CAPTCHA,
Delta Poetry Review— Cumulus Clouds, Clarke County, Georgia,
First Literary Review – East – Color Fields,
Journal of Radical Wonder – Chinese Mustard, Fountain Pens Will Improve Your Life, Great Blue Heron, Lauds, Trout Fishing Warwoman Creek, Georgia,
Last Stanza Poetry Journal – Learning How to Sing, Picking Carrots, Snow Melt,
MacQueen's Quinterly – Daylilies, First Cicada, For the Girl at the Book Fair With the Crematorium Tote, Heart Cracked Not Broken, Joys of Gardening, Mindfulness, Oh You Rascal Billy Collins, Seven Sisters, The Gravity of Impulse, Wakefulness,
Medusa's Kitchen – Ambivalent About Crows, Clicking on the Heart, Colonoscopy, Lessons from the Zen Poet, Off-Blue Sky, The Couch, DeKaye's Brown Snake, The Constellations, Missed Opportunities, Seminole Pumpkin,
Moss Piglet – Sketchy Old Man,
One Sentence Poems – Communalities,
Poetica - Left Over Kugel,

Rust and Moth - Black-Shouldered Kites
Salvation South – Bomb Cyclone in Athens, Georgia, Paying Attention on the Baldwin Grade, Quartering an Apple,
Sheila-Na-Gig – The Hours of Prayer,
Song of Eretz – To the Careworn Live Oak Trunk Washed Up on Morro Strand,
Verse Virtual – A Glimmer, Anguish, Aubade With Horny Mockingbird, Beach Lots, St. George Island, June, California Bay Laurel, Cause Unknown, Do We Really Need Another Poem About the Ocean?, Fish Market, Grandpa's Tackle Box, Longleaf Pine Bark, Make the Barbies Talk, Daddy, The Sisters,
Wild Roof – The Emotions of Trees,
Your Daily Poem – Gramma's Strudel,

CONTENTS

I.

Snow Melt

The January thaw fools us all,
merely land's false labor and spotting,

because a full-term spring gestates
until April—precocious ones

late March—when Sol's cleansing finally
dissolves winter's ivory caul. Streamside

in the hollers, the thaw reveals
both Jacob and Esau—tea green buds

and last year's fisher-trash—blue worm boxes,
vape cartridges, corn cans, empty chaw

pouches. Bloodroot and bluets lay
entranced under a soil quilt, and

mountain laurel and rhododendron
blossoms just sweet woolgatherings

of the piney mountains to the west.

2.

In the Sixteenth Century, artist
Giuseppe Arcimboldo painted

aristocrat's faces composed of
fruit, veggies, and grain. Did ergot

give him such license? Wouldn't vermin
have been more accurate—that era being what

it was? Rats and lice our true brethren,
and human history a continuous

dry heave of disease, exploitation, and calamity.

3.

Last September tenth, I said I loved you
and watched an empty wave break across

your face. Five weeks later, my us-memories
were icicles bleeding out in the thaw.

When I looked around our—I mean my—
bedroom, all that remained were your two

Charleston souvenir ashtrays and a
sleeveless cranberry tee.

4.

April tenth—typical thaw. But every
spring, the land grasps me and says "true

portraits can't be painted with sweet plums
and honey, or rats and lice alone—we

all require something in-between."

Seven Sisters

For thirty seconds at ten pm
time held its breath—Emma striding
away, an ebb tide on Clayton street.
her auburn hair and rust-colored
scarf, small waves in the October
wind, until finally, she's eclipsed
by the parade of college kids
bar-hopping—it's Thursday night after
all—their pockets graced by fake
IDs and credit cards billed
to Mom. No prof is foolish
enough to teach on Fridays,
when all those quotes about the
"love that burns brightest", "hottest",
"scorches", "sears", float by—lyrics
from a mental karaoke
machine, and today being just short of my
thirty-eighth birthday, I stepped out
of the revolving ten pm sky
full of twinkling co-eds, and ran my
fingers over the two burn scars on
my left bicep—wondering why I
couldn't keep that flame burning,
wondering how my heart had twisted
into the Pleiades—those seven
star sisters that can't be viewed
directly, always hovering on the
the periphery—just out of
focus—never crisp, never clear—
never to be held.

Paying Attention on the Baldwin Grade

Passing the big Ingles market I speed through the last intersection in Baldwin Georgia, and crest the ridge holding up the South end of town, only to find the undulating Piedmont hills laid out before me—visibility at least twenty-seven miles—odd for July, with its shower-curtain humidity, even though white and red oaks do their best sets of push-ups provisioning oxygen, while loblolly and shortleaf pines comp us with chasers of pinene, the real deal, not that fake Christmas tree hanging from your rear-view mirror, and I am gobsmacked by the immensity and continuity of this robust green landscape, distant from the ocean, yet looking like nothing so much as a horizon-long set of large rollers from a mid-Atlantic storm, so many waves of yellow-green, green-green and blue-green, colors ebbing and flooding with the breeze, like some window shade that you pull down but keeps rolling itself up, and I should really pull over and suck it all in like a long toke on a joint—let this immensity fill my lungs and seep into iron-red arterial blood for a lap or two around my body, but this is where the eight mile stretch of forty-five ends and we're back up to sixty-five within two-thirds the length of the local high school football field—my wife and daughters are accustomed to my speeding, not too fast mind you, just the six or seven mph of lagniappe the troopers give you, and Georgia 441 takes speed so well, as long as you slow up on the unbanked esses just north of Homer where you have to drop to sixty if there's traffic, but when no one's on your right, you can slalom across the lanes, drifting like Mario Andretti at the Grand Prix of Monaco—windows down and chestnut hair flapping—and that dendroid diorama of big mid-oceanic waves stays with me, all the way to Athens as I inhale the citrus flavor of new sourwood flowers, and drop down to sixty-two at the Clarke County speed limit sign—while my neurons write this second, this minute, this hour, in my every grinning cell.

A Glimmer

Planting a garden is revolution—
hope triumphing over despair. Flower
or veggie—all green comes from a smoothie
of crushed rock and humus—spiked with
nitrogen, phosphorous, and micronutrients.

Even seed anatomy amuses—the coat
that keeps all dry and warm, cotyledon,
the battery for growth, hypocotyl
and plumule--stem and shoot, and last
the embryonic root, the radicle,
linking us to the first revolution.

Seeds are small packages of optimism.
Decisions that light and warmth will prevail
and jonquils or turnips, lilies or peppers
will rise, one or both. There is hope in
nourishing life besides our own—faith
in clear skies and sun, that spring is the pupa
of summer and summer fall. That hope can
be cultivated more easily than cut down.

What Young is Too Young

to hold responsible, when the brain
isn't fused till 25? Sorting debris

in the rear-view mirror of life, I
apologize to Chris C., my first

real girlfriend—someone who picked up
hurt sparrows, patching bloody

wings and tails—including me
at sixteen.

2.

Red pixie haircut, thin hips and breasts
kissed with Cherokee rose, she was

a colt tossing its head in spring
sunlight. But my chest had holes that
only could be filled by the wet heat
of new skin against my own.

3.

Her parents served us espresso
and anisette after our dates, and

I was stunned by how a happy home
was just a nod and quiet smile, which

makes my spurning of Chris even
less understandable—but I was too

young to know that misery is
a bowl that eventually can be

emptied.

Leftover Kugel

Not really noodles, Pesach--
a week of remembered
sacrifice—sure, the cellophane
wrapper read Pareve for
Passover. Bland and chewy,
texture like old camel saddles.
Remembered sacrifice.

Not for eating plain, or even
topped with moguls of parmesan
cheese, but drowned in butter, egg,
sugar, pineapple, and cinnamon—
then baked at 350 in Gramma's
rectangular cake pan, it melds
into a Pesach kugel to die for.
Pareve kugel, our people's
offering for unleavened dessert.

My tongue buds say "sweet, umami,
a hint of salt—the perfect foil
for 7AM dark roast after
an evening with four cups.
Remembered sacrifice,

and the sacred act of living
in the here and now. This coffee,
this kugel.

Chinese Mustard

Tangy, smoky, musky, all apply, as I close my eyes
and inhale—just slightly—shoulders tensed in memory
of a large whiff mistakenly taken thirty-seven years
ago, and my chair-upsetting bathroom race to return
red-daubed eyes to blue.

I am older now and more circumspect.

As fumes darn the air above the saucer, my nose wrinkles—
neurons firing, while the backs of my eyelids screen scenes
from Tang and Song dynasties—flowing silk dresses in mint,
and salmon, and thick yellow tunics the color
of new corn.

Melding the mustard with soy, achieving the proper Dao of
texture and heat, has the illicit feel of a first caress, while suimei,
quiver gently in the woven bamboo steamer, and await the
sauce.

Fillings

1. Best in town/my dentist/the bonus/a mere three-block walk.

2. Waiting clothes me ungracious/first appointment of the day, always.

3. Today, replacing fillings/an endurance test of four/ love the dentist / hate his trade.

4. Walking over/ hands of morning fog push hard against my chest/return home?

5. So many unpleasantnesses/chant of the grinding rasp/ aroma of burning enamel/ gritty rinse-water/staff gossip/punch of seating a new filling.

6. He takes my blood pressure, "it's high"/big effing surprise, and finally asks, "Valium next time?"

7. Bless his heart.

Anguish

Something moves on the sidewalk, writhing,
like butter across a red-hot griddle,
while post-storm steam swirls upwards like the
gyre of turkey vultures riding August-
afternoon thermals.

The worm turned left not right, and now lies
on a concrete stove-top, rather than
lounging in the rain-drop bower of
zoysia grass.

A "lower" creature, I know. Non-
sentient—no real nervous system, but
clearly in distress. Darwin would let
fate play leading man—
not me.

Sliding a fish hook through their coelom
I don't cringe—there is purpose in that
pain, but here there is none. I sigh and
use thumb and index finger to pitch
the worm far onto the
wet grass.

Today's jog will be spent saving worms—
bending from the waist is a good stretch.

Ambivalent About Crows

1. My heart a pendulum—crow love to crow hate—and back again—these large, dark Einsteins—bulling everyone from Carolina Chickadees to Red-Bellied Woodpeckers—despots of my yard—they guard and hoard the suet block, like a hockey goalie fronting the net.

2. Darwin said, "I get it, aggression is good—fight for survival and all that—pass on those traits" although it took Watson and Crick to figure out the trick— with a side of Mendel's peas—back to the main path—crows.

3. The corners of my mouth turn upwards in admiration—then arc downwards—biological referee raising the head crow's left wing in victory—eleven species now defeated in our yard.

4. Another meaningful friendship lost?—crows have great memories and I've shooed them repeatedly—my picture tacked onto the murder's "unwanted" bulletin board—beware of the mean dude on Highland Avenue—yes, social transmission of knowledge—it's a fact—they remember faces, and their parents—solve a puzzle, no problem—even tool use—much to respect.

5. I can do a great caw, and if unseen, lure them close for a corvid—"who's the new bird"—but at first sight—I'm marked as avian fraud not friend.

6. Can amends be made—perhaps more peanuts on the porch?

The Couch

The couch cools my thighs for the first time in four months given that fucking Summer has left the building, and no I don't mean my ex, who liked to "stuff the taco" on this anti-vegan, 8 foot, cowhide-covered, living-room filler—it's true my heart raced to her little moans and quick inhalations which complimented the squeaks her tanned ass made when it rubbed against the ten-year old leather, but that's old news— dried up tears and cracked heart—two years later she's just a slightly faded image stored somewhere in my left eye—but what makes my heart race today—yes, a bit sad—is the elation I feel from the Georgia Bulldog's comeback win in the fourth quarter of last night's game—having been ten points down to Mizzou in the third quarter—and deep down I do agonize over the fact that I'm conflating hot sex and football—the anticipation—the foreplay—and finally—the climax. But four quarters are about all I'm getting' these days.

Fish Market

Sorted on ice—an Expressionist
palette of rockfish reds and oranges
flare, but the greens and blues of skipjack
and bonito dominate like good
waves at Rincon, while doormat flounder
sport a yin-yang of espresso top and
creamy underside.

A memory of La Boqueria, just
off the Ramblas in the Barrio
Gothico, Barcelona's old town,
old like zero CE, Common Era
that is, a less inciting marker
than Anno Domini. Every fish
kiosk holds constellations of species,
maybe thirty apiece.

Shot-glass eyes, gaping mouths and fiery
dermis signify beasts from light-swallowing
depths, mostly rockfish but an exotic
or two like orange roughy, now
overfished—odd flat barrel shape
and clan membership—the slimeheads.
Who knew they lived two-hundred years?

Boom and bust describes many things.

But in Athens, Georgia, the Kroger
resists whole fish, just fillets and steaks
presented—unclad muscles, gray-white to
pink—myomeres now released from bone
and scales, sad as a leafless forest,
or black fungused stalks of corn.

I remember Gramma's halting steps—
opening our back door for Newman
the Fish Man, who delivered blue pike
from Lake Ontario's thirty meter
isocline, shallow water perch that
fried up light as clouds in June
and bass, striped with the salted smell
and taste of a Long Island beach.

When did we unplug the world—build
that synthetic wall of cinder block
and mortar, slip into our vacuum-sealed
bed for safety and comforting warmth?
Was it puberty, adulthood or
parenthood?

I wipe a few grains of river sand
from my eyes, and hope for the
tap-tap-tap on my line.

Seminole Pumpkin

Gardening twenty years, I've
given up planting squash—all hope
exhaled from years of defiled
stems. Vine borers—like so much
Old South—veneer of oaken
courtesy—over a hollow, angry, core.

Then a friend said "Seminole
Pumpkins"—historic gift of Calusa,
Seminole, and Creek—seeds planted
at the bases of pines and oaks—they
watched vines snake-up twenty plus
feet—pumpkins dangling like party
lights on a humid August night.

Toes bathed in dew—I walk
to the garden, to find foot-wide leaves
the color of fast chlorophyll,
guarding seven ripening
green-streaked pumpkins

"Chassahowitzka" the Seminoles
said—"hanging pumpkin", now
also river, and region.

Like many gifts, this one is
undeserved, but given anyway.

To the Careworn Live Oak Trunk Washed Up on Morro Strand

If the world hadn't called me away—injecting knowledge
and career, I'd be with you now, resting quietly on
your trunk, tranquility rolling over my limbs—a salving
fog—do others feel your emanations or is it all
just ether from my lungs?

In my beach year I sat every evening, embraced
by your second branch from the end—the solid one—me
looking edge-ward where ocean licked sky.

Storms teach us both the necessary and accessory.

Anchored atop a finger bluff—fifteen feet above the
spring tide line—did you insult Neptune only to be flung
up here in gang-banger impetuosity, or
perhaps it was a rogue wave spawned four hundred and
twenty seven miles mid-ocean—regardless, what a
view you have—on mica-thin winter days Hawaii is almost
within my grasp, and I imagine psychedelic fishes,
afternoon breezes tart as just-ripe pineapples, and all the
poi my lank stomach will hold.

I've dropped by again—been too long I know, but time
never exceeds the speed limit, and here you are, still
resting on the strand—unaged by both our year together
and the ten years since—perhaps the Appalachian love
ballads I sang you out of loneliness, aided your stability.

Both algebra and full hearts require constants.

Communalities

Bats do that at times,
flap into my thoughts
then careen around my brain,
till I find some way
of setting them free,
ink—

wet,

on a shiny page.

II.

Quartering an Apple

What does it mean to slice up fruit,
to disassemble an organic
universe into parts, dismemberment
not from anger or spite, but merely
for ease of consumption—four
slices set skin down like unfooted
salad bowls, wobbling slightly back
and forth, as I pick up the plate.
You can—sorry, you may—quarter any
apple with the same result. Winesap,
Delicious, Mackintosh, even the new,
sweet as a spring sunrise, Lemonade
apples I bought at the rusty nail-
stained fruit stand, on the four-lane,
South Carolina Route 25, between
Greenville and Asheville.

Didn't Isaac plead with Abraham "but
isn't the whole more than the separated
parts?" And if he was sacrificed,
would our people have been the first
quarter removed from the G-dhead? Which
circles back to the planetary
shape of apples and Eve's desire for
that first taste, and my odd curiosity
regarding which type of apple she
chose? Do religions agree to
disagree about this? Did she choose

Catholic-sweet like the Lemonade, or
Wiccan-tart like a Fuji? Jewish-
long-lasting like an Arkansas Black,
or Puritan-bitter like the thick skin of
a Granny Smith?

What would physics say about all of this?

The Quiet

Rising before the sun
I leave the bed softly,
my beshert unstirred,
then tread across slate-blue
Spanish tiles, their cool-breathe
unseen in the dark.

Every day is filled with leaves
we never unfurl—though they
tell us we are loved.

And the hour before dawn is
a silk jacket, if you chose to
extend your arms.

I make the coffee, pouring
hot water over grounds dark
as burnt oak. It is a slow dance
in the unlight, demanding
patience and steady hands,
as the first beams enter the
eastern kitchen window.

The coffee rested, I
pour a cup and return
to bed, pillows propped up
against our white-worn
headboard.

My wife shifts—her right leg
now touching mine as I
sit, drinking black coffee,
in the dark.

Learning How to Sing

Ears truly open / you hear the Earth's voice.
A baritone / geologic depth and range.
Birch leaves unfurl in the key of G
while samaras of red maples drop

in A minor / waving farewell to
lower branches / April breezes run
scales ending at high C / raising
hairs on my forearm.

Ears closed / missed notes and options
manifold "shoulds" / vacations not taken / condos
unpurchased / the child that could have been.
Life's tune wafts away / ten minutes late / dropped

call / tire flat as a road-killed skunk
turn right not left / shrills like A or C sharp.
Singing lessons mean open ears / breath
shakes joy oi oi oi oi oi oi loose

from vocal chords / then zing, zing, zing,
zing, zo, zo, zo, / my notes in blissful
synchrony with teacher's ivory keys.
For twenty minutes I live in a waved

universe of perfect vibration / no me, no you /
just notes clasped close.

Off-Blue Sky

So I asked the sky, who responded in a nettlesome voice, "that's Sky, capital S", "what makes you special, I mean all those photos, paintings, poems and descriptive phrases?" and they replied "everyone's got it backwards, it's not Earth that holds us in place—we're the glue holding that glob of rock and dirt together—Earth hates that reality. In fact, we stop her from rolling down the astral bowling lane right into the Sun—which would leave humanity twisting and popping like bacon in hot cast-iron. We secure her in endless pirouettes, like a baton twirler on the varsity squad. And those show offs, the Oceans—they steal their color from us, okay, exaggeration—though mostly true. But is there anything that unites people more than the sight of us in a cobalt dress—I mean I'm everywhere from Tierra del Fuego to Greenland, as are our blushes—yellow to crimson sunrises and sunsets? When Earth harangues, I turn cloud-grey and tear up—when exhausted, fog arrives—but anger brings the purples and greens of tornados and typhoons.

I'm really much more sensitive than I seem."

The Constellations

So Zeus immortalized his BFFs—
throwing handfuls of diamonds across
the black velvet cloth of night.

Castor and Pollux—two brothers, one
murdered, one alive—now the twinned
corpus—Gemini.

Mega-mammals, Taurus and Ursa
Major—one a philandering Zeus'
and the second his lover,
transformed by righteous Hera—
both walk Autumn skies.

Pegasus, sprung from Medusa's
slain body—now Neptune's steed
Orion, the Heaven's hunter,
and sea God's son.

Stories all—that warm November
nights.

Surrounded by patterns—but
what do we see?

Last January the Virgin Mary waved
hello from my pre-bed-time cocoa.

Or perhaps it's all just *apophenia* –
the spider web the brain spins denying
randomness—patting my forearm to
say—"I will turn this into something safe."

Make the Barbies Talk, Daddy

1.
Our kids don't sleep, so we stumble through
the days. A bedroom brood chamber,

queen (us), single (five year old), and
crib (baby), while clean laundry in

the blue latticed basket shouts
"fold me" as it squats in an unclogged

square meter of bedroom, but there's
no room for a body to sort

clean boxers, so I wear nylon
gym shorts—washed daily, in our

soaped, porcelain white bathroom sink.

2.
We climb the hours until bedtime,
our PhDs granting knowledge

and fretful thoughts, as we navigate
the minefield of our home. Eyeless toes

step lightly over homeless pacifiers
and Legos strewn across red oak floors

like a modern version of Van Gogh's

sunflowers. Some breaths are half

taken, as we shrug, and another
furrow joins the quartet at lip's corner.

3.
I'm an only child raised by a
single Mom—now a father—young girls

and rhinestones a mystery, though my
wife—youngest of six—navigates

this sea of girlness like a homing
salmon, zig-zagging through 21st

century seas. Masters of class
rooms, our tools—logic and analysis

mostly fail with these girls. Some
dilemmas ethical—should we or

shouldn't we buy the requested
Barbies? Scientist Barbie makes

the cut, as do Latinx Engineer,
and African-American physician

Barbie. Mom said "a boy—no dolls".

4.
Nightmares run through our beds again, and I'm
empty as the valves of a shucked oyster.

But it's time to animate the
Barbies and I'm clueless, and dead

tired. Moving to Rachel's room, my
back against her bed—we sit on the

blue-grey braided rug, a Barbie
in each hand and she says in a

slightly irritated, bird voice "make
the Barbies talk, Daddy. Make them talk."

So I am pushing through my weariness,
plumbing the depths of creativity,

and I morph Barbie One into a surgeon
performing an appendectomy, while

Barbie Two quickly earns a PhD
in astrophysics and begins lecturing

on black holes. I amuse Rachel for
five minutes and forty-two seconds—

then she says "that was okay, but now
let's change their outfits".

Gramma's Strudel

I walk up our glassy steps, wet-clothed
and red-cheeked from the cold slap
of January tenth, and an after
school snowball fight with the seventh
and eighth grade bullies from Addison
Avenue, their aim deadly from two
years of pony-league play.

Twisting the knob I'm caught by
an eddy of cinnamon, allspice,
prunes, raisins and shelled walnuts.

It is strudel weather and Gramma is baking.

A four-foot-nine relic from the Nineteenth
Century, born before fortified
cereals and cheap multi-vitamins.
Survivor of Ukrainian pogroms
and third-class ocean passages.

Gone, these forty years.

All those leaves I've let fall
from my family tree—neglect,
youthful hubris, early deaths,
and more.

If only I could remember
her recipe.

Joys of Gardening

I walk out to the back-yard garden, four double-dug beds, sheathed in six-foot high anti-deer, plastic mesh, which should really be eight feet but like my current belly, the stuff folds over on itself, but it's still okay, (the fence, not my belly), because it doesn't work so much by being stronger than 125 pound deer, but via their lack of ability to see or smell it, and deer detest things they can't sense, and don't try to knock them down, which has saved my garden for the last fifteen years when I first had to put up a fence, because these neighborhood rats on stilts have lost all fear of humans, and saunter to and fro through our back yard, and in summer instruct their frolicking white-spotted fawns how best to destroy our flowers, shrubbery, and veggies, and I'm thinking back to that spring night fifteen years and two weeks ago, when in one night those rats took out an entire seventeen by five foot bed of various lettuces: little gem, red oak leaf, Batavia, trout, red sails, black seeded Simpson, red cos, and bibb—a bed that was as intricate and colorful as a piece of millefiori glass from Murano, and all gone sometime between midnight and six am, which led to the genesis of the first fence. Today is July 27th, so lettuce passed its finals and put away its books two months ago, and today the garden sports typical summer vegies, cherry tomatoes, red, green, and sweet banana peppers, ichiban eggplant (Japanese for "the best"), rattlesnake pole beans and dragon's tongue bush beans. However there is a missing vegetable report out for squash, which I haven't grown in at least a decade, because the squash vine borers eat that shit up like a sorority girl on a sushi date where the bf is paying—hence, no zucchini, no patty pan, no standard-bearer of the South, the yellow crookneck, but in a pity-purchase a few years back I bought a hand-made pack of heirloom Seneca Pumpkin seeds from the daughter of a friend who also is a famous writer, a kindness really because we all like to support each other's kids, and the package was cute as a 12-year old's pink baby-doll pajamas—and I bought them, thinking all the while of those fucking vine borers, which actually are the larvae of a quite attractive, orange and black Halloween costumed moth and last year I threw a few out in an open patch in the flower bed on a lark and fuck me if they didn't sprout and produce a few squash, before those long-legged rats ate every leaf off the plant. The squash were damn good and now I've planted them in bed three but they are taking over the entire garden, I guess nine seeds in three hills was simply too much, and they're about to climb the deer fence, which wouldn't be a problem except I don't think the netting is strong enough to support the two pound squashes, and I read somewhere that you could make slings for them out of nylon stockings, but who wears nylons any more, especially here at the south end of North Georgia where climate change can make even May show her triple digits, and at this point I'm just struggling with how to handle these over-achieving squash plants.

Mindfulness

And Scott says, "you know, down by the power station on South Lumpkin, just before we turn off on Westlake" and I think what the fuck there's no power station on South Lumpkin, but I say nothing, because Scott is the only person I can get to run with me daily, and twenty-two hours later at mile one point two five I don't hang a left on Westlake and instead continue down South Lumpkin to QA/QC his statement, and fuck me if he isn't right, there is a power station just past where we turn on Westlake, though it's hidden behind a lapstrake fence, stained the color of oak and hickory trunks, but this camouflage is undone by the topping of rolled concertina wire like frosting on a cupcake, as if a prison were a cupcake, which leads me to the point that all kinds of shit is going down around us, all of the time, and some of it blurs by because of inattention and speed, like that power station which I've been driving past for the last thirty-eight years and others are missed because they're equivalent to that constellation with seven stars that you can only see out of the corner of your eye, even though you try all sorts of squints to bring it into crisp focus, but it's always just out of reach, like happiness or fidelity.

Which brings me to the point of this discussion, besides apologizing to Scott, who in truth can be both wrong and bull-headed, and that is to paraphrase Gautama Buddha "pay the fuck attention", don't just let trees and birds float by randomly like abandoned plastic bags caught by the wind—I mean what kind of trees are those, because their identities are like Matryoshka dolls—tree, oak, post oak, sand post oak, and so on down to individual cells which maybe even have first and last names in the botanical phone book. And birds—we're on the Eastern Flyway so during spring and fall migration there are hundreds of species and saying "oh, it's just some warbler" really is a mortal rather than a venial sin, not that any priest is going to scourge you for saying it.

And so the next day I'm out there running at seven thirty in the morning, because it's going to be in the high nineties, and I turn left on Westlake and then left on Milledge Terrace and I'm paying attention to the water oak and chalkbark maple on the right and spot a whitetail doe with two fawns, here in the middle of fucking town, eating daylilies out of a flower bed right up against a thirties red brick house, and I crash into a parked '09 Audi hatchback and cut both my thigh and calf—and now I'm on my way to the St. Mary's emergency room for at least seven stitches.

Nah, just kidding: aside from that effing power station I really am quite mindful.

Missed Opportunities

Heading north to the western
Blue Ridge—shielding California
cousins from August in Georgia.

Kids strapped in, we're an hour down the road,
when the afternoon thunderstorm rhumbas
in, flexes twice, and spews three inches

of soupy rain. Having driven this road
for seventeen years, I'm on autopilot,
then I notice a box turtle trying

to cross both lanes of this curved knife, that
slices through piney forest—roadside sourwoods
decked with glowing yellow flower spikes.

Rain halted, steam swirls from pavement—
heat wraiths—while this Triassic relic
plods on. Red eyes tell me his pronouns are

he/him—he's halfway across, and I
pull our Subaru to the shoulder,
to begin the rescue.

Whoosh—a car approaches, maybe
50, 55—quick swerve—a hollow
pop—a sound like an old pumpkin
being smashed.

Turtle parts explode like brown fireworks—
an unbidden scene comes to mind—Mom's
loud scream as her Karmen Ghia vaults
the thirty-foot embankment on Baja
Highway One, just outside Tecate.

Never miss a chance to say "I love you".

Aubade with Horny Mockingbird

Since 4AM he's been going
through his bootleg catalog
cardinal chirps, metal band
grackle, and chipping sparrow
trills.

Unmated males sing at odd
hours, bills leering at
all that moves, even cars.

Hope slides in on the second
beam of every sunrise, even
though last call was ten days past.

5:37AM and he's still pleading.
True dawn an hour away—
but work-thoughts climb
over the fading fence of
sleep.

Trout Fishing, Warwoman Creek, Georgia

May ninth, and the stream defenses are up
rows of *Leucothoe*—dog hobble,
like emplacements at a WWII
battlefield: they rise up the bank
until the soil is hard and dry as
my fifth-grade teacher, Miss Sheaffer
(that D in penmanship unwarranted,
even in 1964).

Evergreen foliage—serrations
worthy of Solingen knives—the name
apt—hobble—"to strap, to tie together",
stems embracing—a cool, stubborn
emerald quilt. Oblong leaves—flower
clusters hang—a carillon of ivory
bells pushing malevolence—
"you shall not pass."

Thirty-seven yards later I weave
through a gap—drop into a knee-high
riffle—the water fifty-two degrees.

Childish boss and two mortgages—the
trout help me leave my hobbles behind,
but the tether is long and tensile.

Seasonal Affective Disorder

It's day nine of gray skies, clouds stacked
in layers like a torte made with
fourteenth century flour from some
terra-cotta urn, then layered
with whipped cream past its sell-by.

For the first few days, December clouds
bring a smile, just a slight upturn of
mouth corners. Fall has left the building,
and Winter's disparate hues are a
painting by Whistler, white on silver,
silver on ash, ash on cream.

Sometimes the December ground hugs
itself so hard that fog erupts—a
cloud reaching upwards rather than down.

By day five I'm trying to peel this ashy
veil off my skin—this epidermal
ply of annual depression, my own
personal unmerry-go-round, with
day five of ashy skies so demanding
it scrapes every red and yellow off
my jacket.

Then a small gap of blue appears
like a book whose place I've lost, but
somehow reopens to exactly
the right page, and small thanks travel
via nerve and artery from eyes to heart.

Grandpa's Tackle Box

The thickened air was cold as
permafrost as we picked through
87 years of accumulation,
sentimental trilobites wrapped in
the papery shale of lived years.

In a far corner, under an eave,
sat a tackle box: metallic green
mottled with rust, the colors of
duckweed trapped in the corner of
a pond full of brim.

Opened, the layered trays creaked—joints
almost as frozen as Grandpa's
aged knees. The box was a small
galaxy of rusted hooks, bobbers,
plugs and needle nose pliers.
The tangle brought back his hours of
help with my middle school science
project, a model cell—Golgi bodies,
mitochondria, and the sticky
sounding endoplasmic reticulum.

An embalmed night crawler lays across
both a red-headed bass plug and a
leopard frog endowed with two trebles,
somehow having escaped our old tin
worm can. It crumbled at my touch.

My earliest memory, us walking back
from Uncle Jake's pond. I didn't
even reach four feet and he remarked
"The stringer's heavy, let me carry it.
We had a good day, didn't we?"

Fountain Pens Will Improve Your Life

Attraction thrives on the unique—individual, object, or location—even small and inanimate objects like my vintage fountain pens—first purchase 1976, a late Thirties, Parker Parkette, black celluloid that warmed in the hand, gold-plated fittings and barrel engraved "Dr. Schwartz"—eternally grateful, dude. Profound ruminations leapt from its nib, while I stepped one, two, three; one, two, three; through the PhD waltz, then advanced to faculty, where after two years I uncovered plated colleagues, whose worn ten carat exteriors exposed minds of pot metal, and wanton academic desires, pleas for free lectures and coauthorships—forgive me for straying from the main point, it's the candor brought on by my only weeks-away retirement gold watch—ha ha, as if—but looping back to the black Parkette, it was my first possession from the Jazz Age, and sat proudly in the chest pockets of my seasonal California wardrobe—Penny's tees and Sears flannels—forty-years on I'm stylin' the same—higher quality pens and threads, though.

I am a better man for fountain pens. *Mindful*: the nib of my twenties Waterman 52 Ripple glides across the letter tablet calming both heart rate and breathing—my thoughts ease into the tanned arms of this exact moment—inhalations and exhalations unconsciously purposeful. *Thoughtfulness*: pondering the next line, I rotate the pen slightly to the left, accentuating variation in the letters—thin horizontals and broad verticals—a visual treat uplifting lonely recipients of hand-written letters. *Patience*: my hand slows and steadies, birthing visual clarity. *Humility*: ink stains seep over thumb, index, and middle fingers—sapphire blue today, green, brown, and red on the morrows—ink surviving showers and multiple hand washings. "Are you an artist", "no, I just like to write with old fountain pens". *Diligence*: like my heart, fountain pens need daily exercise.

Beach Lots, St. George Island, June.

7:23 am and the morning sun
pries sweat from scalp and forehead,
a saline poor-man's spa, it runs into
my eyes and stings almost as much as
seeing new subdivided lots only
92 yards from the high tide line.

They've been dozed, but indigenous plants
say "not so fast", and even some sand pines
are left, to karate chop the breeze. Beach
sunflowers match the chrome-yellow, eastern
orb—every name has a maritime preface
here in the Eastern Panhandle, from random
clumps of sea oats that resemble Dad's
scalp after chemo, to the white trumpets
of beach morning glories trying to climb
the laid PVC sewer lines sticking
up through sugar-sand like the tips of a
fossilized plesiosaur that crawled
up on the beach to die, but these "bones"
presage Lexus wagons and sockless loafers.

This land is residual, the "forgotten
coast", and many things sport a broken face,
especially Gramma Earth—strewn with
beer cans and scraggly plastic bags from
the Pig. Yesterday, I parked my Highlander
next to a Bentley rag-top, oxymoronically
sitting at the Dollar Store, which sells

produce because food deserts aren't just in
cities. The driver was sheathed in a Red
Sox jersey and had one of those chi
chi pony tails that looked like the
ass-end of a sow in October. His face
twisted into a sneer worthy of
De Niro as I slowly opened my
paint-chipped door, making sure to leave
a half-court of air between our vehicles.

He was looking at a flyer for beach lots.

Colonoscopy

In politics, it ain't the crime, it's the cover-up—but in digestive medicine, it ain't the procedure, it's the prep—Go-Lyte, sarcasm?—because nothing about this is lyte, and somewhere there's a research pharmacist meaner than a hung-over preacher on Monday morning. It's three o'clock on a mid-July afternoon—two tablets of bisacodyl—the pre-game warm up. Sadly my GI doc has denied my request for an early start—"research shows…"—I drink my first quart of Go-Lyte at six PM—now, my three-hour reign on the commode—a second fucking quart at two AM—begetting an additional reign from two fifteen to four AM—all of this, after one day with just white rice and unseasoned chicken, the next just clear broth and jello—no red or purple, mind you—right now my stomach begs for the Chinese buffet, but I lay on the couch, waiting for the next bathroom sprint, limp as a garden string bean, left out in the July 17th sun, watching old Andy Griffith reruns, but fuck it, it's worth it—colon cancer, ooops, colorectal cancer to be precise—mortality cause number three for non-smoking males.

Afterwards, I learn three polyps were knocking on the door of my colonic epithelium, despite the no solicitors sign. They had no inkling, they were headed for the reaper via cold snare—twisted little fuckers that they were—modern medicine is great—as is the sausage biscuit and black coffee from Momma's Boy, I'll eat in the Volvo—wife driving, while I mumble, "wasn't bad, but that prep."

Lessons From the Zen Poet

Having written for years I finally
visited the Zen Poet, and asked
about his work—he said "nothing new—
been working on the same poem for
a decade; almost have the wording
right."

Five years later I returned and he
replied "wording finally right,
working now on line structure."

Five years later I returned
to find him rearranging stanzas
and whispering "not yet".

An additional five years
yielded "punctuation
still isn't quite right. And
I exclaimed, but Sensei
no one will know your
work, your perfect poem.

He replied "it doesn't matter."

III.

Lauds

5:15 AM—my bladder
whispers "to the bathroom"—but
but it's September-dark, sun
lazier and more languid each
new morning. My wife, asleep on
her left side, shifts and rocks once, as if
the mattress had only absorbed part
of her dream. The room is warm, though
the skin on her upper thighs is cool,
as I lift my arm off her sleeping
stomach. Our local alarm clock,
a young male barred owl, calls from
the back-lot hickory—two "who cooks
for you", then a final "who cooks for
you all". Mating season summertime,
yet his year-round calls echo,
unanswered. A small, red-glass vase with
the last sprig of night-blooming jasmine
sits on my dresser, and after one
more exhale, I reckon I'm done
with sleep. An open paperback, face
down, on her white, mid-century-style
nightstand, tells me she was up for at
least an hour—sleeplessness—bane of
Boomers. The new percale top sheet crinkles
as I roll out of bed on my right
side, then cover her with Gramma's
summer quilt. The old mattress retains
my body's impression for a few

seconds—and hopefully fools her
that I'm still there. She rocks once, slightly,
then settles.

Black-Shouldered Kites

Like satisfaction unfurling on
an August day, I watch two kites
hover over a just-harvested
corn-field—marking stray hoppers
and voles, while late-morning thermals
massage away the haze, and driving
north on I-5, glance east and west
to see both Sierra Foothills
and Coastal Range, gilded in late
summer grass, with a scatter of
grey-green live oaks—the Sacramento
Valley resembling nothing so much
as a giant taco—cilantro
strewn randomly on the edges
of these tortilla mountains—the kites
now just flapping wings suspended
in mid-air—reflected in my left
side mirror, shrinking, until they're
just periods typed on a page
of sky, and my brow furrows as I
wonder whether all my deeds
and intentions dispersed into
the universe have shifted this
disheartened planet even a
millimeter—back towards its proper
orbit.

The Sisters

The heat is triple digits even
in California's coastal oak
forest—I've finished mile two of
five, as sweat-salt doilies my shoulders.

Ahead lay "The Sisters"—four immense
bay laurel trees that inadvertently
have built this trail-nook. Sisters who have
gathered and smoothed local air as
if they were pulling taut the sheets
of an unmade sky, leaving nothing
but odors of oregano, thyme,
and lavender—a balm for my
heaving lungs.

I grin, as the gauze of brown air
disappears—a reverse Big Bang—bad
air now collapsing into a thimble-sized,
avoidable mass.

Passing the Sisters, I admire the work
they've done for these last ninety-eight
years.

Soothing all—they ask for so little
in return.

Blessings

Five thirty AM, November eighth,
and my yard owl, a barred male, has
woken me with his high reverb
"who cooks for me", or perhaps it was
the full moon, last night's eclipse—looking
like an abandoned pumpkin hanging
on the black vine of sky—most likely
it was the fall back to Standard Time—
old body slow to adjust—sleep,
elusive once you've woken—maybe
that should be called resleep—while
the sparse silver forest on my arm is
roused by the cold emptiness of our
room—my wife visiting her siblings
minus one across the continent,
and I could kvetch about missing
her—a bit of me gone—together
forty years, it feels like the solid part
of my smile has faded these last few
days, but then I consider the sister-
in-law who passed one month ago,
and what a blessing it is to watch
the moon turn from silver to orange—
hear that owl, unfulfilled, but
still calling—feel the hair on my arm
stand up in the chill of our November
bedroom.

Do We Really Need Another Poem About the Ocean?

I'm tired of reading about the primordial soup.
About fish birthing tetrapods, and how human blood
is salt-twin to both Atlantic and Pacific—an
umbilical cord never cut—endlessly tugging
at lungs and liver, and the literary device
of oscillating waves and tides as penetration.

I'm really not sure anymore.

I just sang a septet of days on St. George Island, each
one repeating a tempered chorus of sun and surf.
Buffet and Aldean own houses here, but it's still
the "Redneck Riviera" more tag holders from
Ohio and Kentucky than Westchester or DC.

Yes, the sand was new cotton and the turquoise water
smelled of rebirth. Wading through half-foot waves to cast,
the sea held me like the ur-Mother that she is,
though whiting and pompano failed to suckle at my bait—
most of them anyway.

Thankfully, sand gnats were still in class,
learning to extract mammal blood through
chitin straws.

Every afternoon, the wind ran her painted fingers
through my silver hair and each evening, my stomach
bulged with lower life forms—oysters and shrimp, chased

with fried flounder, I crossed the twenty-five feet of
hot asphalt to the beach to watch the sun pull a
greenish sheet of salt water over its drowsy head.

The plague has touched so many—perhaps more
ocean poems are needed.

I'm really not sure about anything these days.

Picking Carrots

It's March 18th and despite the hard
freeze last weekend, our carrots exude
a craving for examination and
evaluation--intoxication
emanating from the bed of orange, red
and purple heads poking up through rollers
of crushed pine bark and black soil.

The secrets of root vegetables arouse me.

Always a hidden story, always a
probability.

Seeds sown last October, but winter's
wardrobe was unhemmed, cool, and bright
enough to sugar these painted vegetal fingers.

Now feathery leaves weave the spring breeze,
their scent a lurid promise. I pull the
largest bunch, parting a wave of soil—sand grains
dripping off the root. It is straight, thick and
half a foot long—a clandestine happiness,
like holding a new lover for the first time.

Moving through the bed, I hope for more sticks
of orange candy, not crooked roots—sour as
an old bachelor.

I move to the next patch and wonder,
what secrets the earth will whisper?

Daylilies

Gone missing overnight, now just clipped
off stems, where flowers kissed our eyes
and buds whispered "soon".

Deer.

Rats on stilts, my neighbor Andy calls
them. Carousing our backyards like local
ten-year-olds in pirate hats. Swashbucklers,
fearing naught.

The Captain of our 'hood, an eight-point,
sacked our backyard reforestation—
stripping bark from magnolia and tulip
poplar saplings—his work of a single night,
August 29th.

Deer are the landscape's bad habit, like
Mom's failure to quit smoking. Deer spank
me by ensuring I never have
enough daylily flowers to thicken
my moo shu or hot and sour.

The buds, straining to mature like ninth
graders, are "golden needles" in Cantonese
cuisine. I like them sautéed, sizzling and
speckled with red chili flakes, and
sesame oil.

Four fence posts done, my optimism
conjures buds, both flower and taste, and the
mingling of the two.

Empathy

Second beer with my colleague—recounting some slight—one more COVIDy A-hole sent shit my way—open and shut, really—like the speeding frat boy who flips off the mom and stroller in the middle of the crosswalk—and fuck me, my dude begins with hypothetical excuses for the A-hole—judge and jury both—though he lacks a single scrap of knowledge about this particular sitch—other than the chapter I've written verbally—accurate as a bullseye—although, yes, sometimes I do coat myself with golden beams of sunshine—but it's sad really, given his successes, that he doesn't have the empathy for a compatriot that a tomato plant gets from a quarter inch stake—something to the tune of "yeah, I totally get why you feel that way", or "damn, that sucks"—fuck no, it's BS like "well maybe he recently broke his toe" and "well maybe he was just bitten by fire ants"—and there's a flash, like a sudden electrical surge, and I realize he's actually excusing his own bad behavior—that this isn't some 2022 "judge not lest ye be judged" advice—but a case of self-esteem so low that deep-down, he believes a refusal to disparage bad behavior of others gives his own transgressions a free pass.

How he gets his grades in on time is beyond me.

New Year's Resolution

I've booted carbs from my dietary family—formerly beloved children: pastry, pasta, rice, and bread, now expurgated and currently residing in the food orphanage—adoption later? Perhaps some Daddy Warbucks will chose these orphaned carbs, yet I can't complain about this new Neanderthal diet of ribeye, chicken, and even creamy camembert—okay so that's very modern fat.

Barb boiled a pound of linguini tonight—a New Year's treat—anti-resolution if ever there was one, and while carbsteam loped upwards to the ceiling of our sunflower kitchen, I descended the heart-pine basement staircase for a tub of homemade pesto—entombed for six months in the chest freezer—ever since the genesis of this no-carb diet, which has, in fact, sent hundreds of my abdominal fat cells to either hell or heaven, who can be sure?

And so this New Year's backslide—a slithering Devil's brew of garlic, parmesan, walnuts, basil leaves and virgin olive oil topping linguini, like pines crowning the Sierra—why wasn't my full plate at dinner enough? Why, at 10:15 PM, did I get out of bed, only to return with all the unconsumed pestoed pasta, which I ate sitting in the dark in our queen-sized bed—warm sleeping body at my side, and because it was a new year, I could only chuckle when I dropped a long, oily strand on our just changed flannel sheets.

The only thing I've missed more than carbs, is our kids going off to college, but tomorrow is a new day and carb-free—if I'm lucky.

First Cicada

It's June in the Georgia Piedmont—
magnolias fully in bloom, as if
someone had built trees from sheets of
dark green wax and tipped branches with
porcelain bowls of vanilla ice cream.

The blossoms push out a breeze of
fruity scent—and walking at seven AM
it smells like Coco Chanel left an
open bottle of Number Five perfume
on each front lawn.

Three miles later I walk down my
driveway to the back yard and hear
a metal rod being dragged over
rusty tin. It's the first
cicada of the year.

Oh You Rascal Billy Collins

I was describing my two published poems about cicadas, one about Brood X which emerged in 2021, and the second, on the emergence of our local annual cicadas, a three-stanza, fifteen-line shorty, melding the piercing sucrose of magnolia flowers (*grandiflora*, that is) with the rusty-iron harmonies of the cicada's song, when a gratuitous someone pointed out your instructions in the poem "The Student"—and I'm only slightly paraphrasing here—"avoid words like cicada," which sucked my satisfaction right out the window as if it were the innocent bystander in seat 37C in the latest James Bond movie—and, ego aside—drastically shortchanges these flying noisemakers, a species originating millions of years ago, and my fingers are indenting the padded arms of my chair as I try not to fixate on how your advice is so damaging to the self-esteem of millions of cicadas—when I realize this is just a toss-off line, a poetic device, from someone who doesn't really know cicadas, the annual from the periodic, the North American from the Antipodean (three hundred Australian species alone), and did you know that almost all "plague" cicadas, the periodic ones emerging every thirteen or seventeen years, exist only in Eastern North America, including your home state of New York? I can't help but believe that your relationship to these cornichon to cigar-stub-sized Pleistocene relics is that of annoying August raspers, and can you possibly know that male cicadas use their tymbals to sing—I mean, how can a poet resist a word like *tymbals*, which, *quod erat demonstrandum*, must be used with the word cicada?

Now it's true that adult cicadas really are just looking for a quick fuck—just pass those genes along and "I'm out of here,", the proverbial "wham bam thank you ma'am—but hell, no one expects them to be able to use Tinder. And really, not to overgeneralize, but doesn't that just make them the equivalent of at least half the human race? I know you weren't describing subjects—just non-euphonious words—but *vortex*, another forbidden fruit, also is poetic brilliance to me—and if I were teaching poetry—I'd certainly advise students to stay away from *liver flukes, scrofula,* and the *candiru catfish.*

Deciduous Trees

Every Fall, leaves fall—redundant?
Bad pun?—or nodding head for our
heart-salving need—the consistent
rhythm of nature's tom-tom?
Frost sticks its toe in the door and
leaves turn, scarlet oaks, maples, as if
flocks of cardinals fell out of the sky,
only to be pasted on bare branches—
orange hickories, magenta dogwoods,
and two-faced sugar maples, first
chrome yellow then deepening to the
crimson of well-oxygenated blood.
It is Fauvism at its best
Andre Derain painting pictures every
October twentieth—varying
slightly in hue and saturation
So many childhood memories—raking, then tearing
piles apart with runs and leaps—always
wondering if frozen ground would
thump your breath.
Years churn like butter, but trees
stand fast—always dressing for autumn—rich
colors—not the pastels of spring prom.
Today, my cheeks are painted with
brush strokes of cold air
as I race towards that pile of leaves.

Pentimento

Like oxygen bound by
heme running under our
dermis, like maple sap
flowing under bark, or
peony petals curled
within the bud—what
is essential is both seen
and unseen.

Dissatisfied, the artist
paints over an image—
years later this pre-thought
rises through the upper
layers—visible, first
as a shadow or tracing,
becoming a leafy tree
or smiling child—it is a
pentimento—the unseen
rising to be seen.

Fifty years ago tomorrow
we dug a hole through the
pine-scented turf of the
Angeles National Forest
burying Mom's ashes—
consummating her wish
for an unmarked grave. I
hated her at the time, but
I gave my word.
Gramma said "this will kill me"—
she lived another decade.

Today, I gaze at the thick chestnut
hair, topaz blue eyes, and unattached
earlobes, of my two grown daughters—
pentimentos all—then inhale sharply—
to wish my failings never pierce
their layers of healthy, brilliant paint.

Coastal Redwoods

The chill rose an hour before
I did, and now washes over my
naked legs as I run, wondering
how water and air have the same
touch, despite different parentage,
liquid versus gas—both homogenous
morphs that lick and envelope to
varying degrees.

In the redwoods, the air is dusted
by millions of feathery needles—as
if some roc or other humongous
prehistoric bird had moulted all
at once, and July is a month large
enough to hold this green bank
deposit. At seven-thirty, sunbeams are
do-si-doeing with redwood needles.

Yesterday, we drove from Sacramento—
a week with my five surviving
sibling-in-laws—we discuss burial
of the sixth and oldest—opinions
hot as the triple-digit July
dailies of the great Central Valley—which
is why, despite internet temp checks,
I'm in running shorts, when it's fifty-two
degrees—carry-ons, after all, are
finite vessels.

Where should the urn of ashes go, and
more importantly, where the fuck is it?
Memorial service, funeral mass,
or both? Is there a will, or are we
headed for probate? Five survivors
discuss.

And despite chicken skin—my hazel
eyes find the door to this sacred
grove—trees fifteen hundred years old—
foot-thick bark, shedding insects, and wild
fires—all forms of pestilence—and I
can't help but wonder how each of us
will be felled, and then received?

Targeted Advertising

Still a bargain, I suppose—free Facebook in exchange for incessant ads in your feed—but they can be frightening, or just difficult—Saturday Times crossword difficult—especially when your North Pole suddenly shifts to the west—like last week when my feed burgeoned with ads for women's apparel including "shapers"—some in bondage neoprene—and panties, transparent as the mica chips on the bottom of Sarah's Creek—which led me to worry the app had morphed into some deranged and malevolent artificial intelligence—like the impolite and persistently villainous robot in Robo-Cop—because sheer panties haven't ever been in my playbook, let alone my size—and it took me until the next Tuesday to recall the grrl-creed meme I had played that produced—"if I cut the cord, you probably handed me the scissors", which frankly, was an okay reading—more accurate than most FB data mining memes—and after posting my puzzlement—two old friends replied "we prefer targeted ads", and I thought "what the hell—I guess you never really do know someone else."

The Stocking Truck

Looking up—bankside hemlocks overshot by creamy fingers of alto-cirrus Appalachian clouds—and here's the stocking truck—Fish and Game tech fiddling with fittings, like an octopus rotating a mussel to find the sweet spot, and suddenly two-hundred hatchery-blessed, rainbow trout glide thirty-seven feet from bridge to river, then rocket off, silver tails like windshield wipers on high, after the cheek slap of the river's surface, at which point I feel the tap-tap-tap—hook an eleven-inch stocker—large for July—suddenly I'm surrounded by guys chucking out corn-baits with their spin-casting outfits, not to cast aspersions—bad pun, and the morning has suddenly become a bit too much like current life—bad pun—with some folks inhaling more oxygen than is ethical, like the thirty-something runner who purposefully bumped me, threatening to knock me off the sidewalk the other day, eyes fixed directly on mine the entire time, a dominance signal right out of Attenborough's African baboons—showing no emotion at all, because others hold no space in such a tiny heart, despite an increased blood capacity from years of exercise, but back to the river, because these dudes have clearly been following the stocking truck—maybe even one is brother-in-law to the driver, because this isn't some random event, but a weekly executed shopping trip, during the March to September stocking season—now there are eight of these dudes standing shoulder to shoulder chucking corn, and I realize I am walking across the glass-like diatom-glazed cobble bottom way too fast, wanting to preserve my six feet of "stream turf", after walking over to the bank to end every fish's suffering immediately, rather than have them flop around and slowly suffocate—suddenly reality intrudes like a great horned owl calling "it's me" at three AM, and I realize I'm headed for a fall—maybe broken bones, and these last two fish aren't worth a hospital cast—bad pun—so I slide-step to the bank, grab my six cooling fish, climb the moss-lined path up to the road, turning downstream (left) to my two secret pools, while evaporating river water cools my legs—after a quarter mile, I part the ivory-flowered branch-tips of rhododendron that roof the stream-side banks, no one here but me and the river, then I lower myself into her cool, uplifted arms.

CAPTCHA

You're an A-hole really,
my optic nerve skewered

far into my cerebellum.
by this chastity belt for

the Web. Postage stamp
pictures, grainier than beach

sand, but missing warmth.

Hacker no, hackee yes,
but minor troubles, once

a laptop purchase—quickly
erased, though the schmuck

reordered sixty-four minutes
later. But you, CAPTCHA,

you've held me hostage
one hundred plus times

Mark all photos with toe
shoes, mark all photos with

with cyanobacteria,
mark all photos with

tires made in Kurume
Japan, mark all photos with a

book title in six point
Gothic.

After three rounds I curse this
century, and then just exhale.

The Gravity of Impulse

When some new thing opens my eyes
I'm a sapling planted in rich, warm
black soil—a granite pebble dropped
into a pond thirty feet deep,
falling faster and faster (I
know—gravity doesn't work that way),
except suddenly, I need to own
every book or piece of equipment
for my new hobby—beginner to
advanced—stone sculpting, watercolor
painting, no-till gardening, until
leaving my study means weaving
my way through skyscrapers made of
unread books.

I'm not good at just dipping my toe
in the water, I'm a whole leg or even
a torso, kinda guy, and I know this
isn't really "healthy"—a word I
frequently ask myself these days,
"is this food healthy", "is this cocktail
healthy", and you might think, at fifty-five
I've learned impulse control and not bought
books one through eight of the latest scifi
series, but gravity doesn't work
that way, and I do love the slightly
acrid smell of new ink on paper,
at least for the six months it takes me
to accept I'll never read these books,

and my hands do tremble just slightly
when I realize that no one can save
you from yourself, because gravity is
a constant, regardless of height or mass.

Walking on Ice at the University of Toronto

Guest lecture and doctoral exam finished yesterday, the table for my Wednesday fun was sadly set with swirling clumps of sky-dandruff, loosed by 40 kph winds (wind-chill -8C)—with heavens silvered like a well-worn nickel. Nevertheless, I portaged west on Bloor St., seeking the Japanese art supply store, and their tablets of fine writing paper. Paper that delights in the purposeful cursive from my vintage fountain pens, as if italic letters were smiling week-old babies. Checking my phone "okay, only a mile from my B&B on Beverely, no problem", although this residence is now just a B—Pandemic cutbacks having removed all things consumable, including coffee—so I'm lucky that Starbucks nests half a block away, on the corner with College. I'm not an ugly American, but reviews are reviews, and I felt like posting a notice on nearby phone poles "B&B, shampoo, bathmat, and bath-towel, missing since Sunday." Yes, I did burn a shit-ton of calories yesterday, walking, in the arctic air, back and forth from Midoco, the art supply store, which did lead to seven consecutive blissful hours of sleep—for this small-town professor, unused to street lights just outside one's double paned window, or carousing students at 2 AM (Why does everyone speak so loudly up here?). But it's now 5:38am on Thursday, and although the corner Starbucks opens at 5:30am—the ground-cake is now covered with tiers of ice topped by snowy frosting, and although my shoe-soles are ground-grippers, walking on this sidewalk is like meeting your ex-in-laws on the street after an ugly divorce, "okay, she cheated, on meeee", and I find myself doing an occasional disco move to maintain balance, while wondering how quickly I can get to coffee, because my skin is tasting that -7C, and I'm jonesing for the tongue coating bitterness of sixteen ounces of dark roast, when it suddenly occurs to me that this is life, isn't it—maintaining balance while slowly moving forward over hazardous terrain, occasional slips and slides, peering in the dark for patches of non-iced concrete, wondering about arrival—progressing—and hoping, all the while, for no hard falls.

For the Girl at the Athens Comic Fair With the Crematorium Advertising Tote

About twice a year, life pokes me right between the eyes, eliminating the 29 greying hairs that form my unibrow. Like today—my first book fair—where I'm hawking my three strikingly different tomes (my latent ADHD no doubt) but the odd truth is that here at the Athens Comic Fair I've sold more gourmet venison cookbooks than graphic novels, and I'm perplexed by the apparently invisible connection between venison cookery and the ink and cosplay of most attendees. Okay, that's snarky and side-eyed, I apologize. So, my just published volume of poetry abuts graphic novel and cook book—old, straight, married, white guy stuff, spiced and colored with the usual dogwood and azalea free verse—a life *in toto* wrapped up in 112 pages, and it's now hour four—my energy flat as the new blacktop on Milledge Heights, but I've made table and parking fees, so who can complain, et voila, she walks by and I notice her tote inscribed with la phrase juste for everything everywhere, right? Witness the evanescent, and transitory nature of all matter, corporeal or not: life, literature, art, and music, all take that last, lung-filling breath, and then—the final swoosh of nothingness.

Sooner or later—we're all part of the burn pile.

Color Fields

The Color-Field painters: Rothko, Still
& Newman, birthed abstract shapes—squares,
fat lines, splotches like dripped candle
wax—colors that contrast &
compliment.

Creative lust is satisfied
by many forms of caress.

I paint with words, hoping to inform
that crimson is a slash of blood, but
scarlet says "please smile."

Today, my mood falls between
viridian & azure—learning
that physics has now established
that light & emotions are one
& the same.

My brain furrows & a query
lingers—is love a particle, or
a wave, or in some essential way,
only complete as both.

IV.

Heart Cracked Not Broken

1. How can I pour the ocean of sorrow into the small cup of my heart?
2. The question for today's year—so much pain—Ukraine, COVID, my sister's miscarriage.
3. How or why, to hold the grief wrapping me like ground fog on a summer's day?
4. I lie down and picture anger-red leaving my body, flowing out my feet—oozing into empathetic air.
5. On every morning run, I feel the spiny specter wisp out my nostrils, then lag further and further behind—smoke from a blown-out match.
6. But tomorrow brings new news, and a cup that must be unfilled every day.

California Bay Laurel

Smell evokes the strongest
memories— bypassing thymus,

racing right to the olfactory
bulb, like some nutso driver in

stop-and-go, passing everyone
on the road's shoulder.

Today I am in the fog of
coastal redwoods, 2500

miles from Georgia's
August oppression—heat

and humidity so bad you
can see fungi grow—sometimes,

even on yourself. So yesterday,
the Tuesday after the funeral

of my wife's oldest sister, we're
hiking in the redwoods and I

am suddenly triggered by a
branch laced with emerald knife blade-leaves,

and instead of the Russian River
Valley, I'm fifteen, standing on

Pacific Coast Hwy One at
Cayucos, thumb out, having just

picked a few bay laurel leaves to
place under my backpack straps—leaves

pushing out the scent of good health—
pungent, peppery, part thyme, part

oregano, somehow slowing my
heart rate—deepening inhalations

and exhalations—injecting a fog
of calm so intense I've forgotten

the thrown objects and occasional
blows of my bipolar mother—

and the oozing wound just to the
left of my heart, sliced by a Dad's

perpetual absence—ghosts
resurrecting phoenix-like, fifty years

later, as I pick leaves from
another bay laurel—when my

cell rings and I hear the voice
of my older daughter, the veterinarian.

Wakefulness

Age 68—uninterrupted sleep an ancient scroll—last week I woke up at two AM—breath racing from running up three flights of stairs to avoid the spectral tsunami soaking floors one and two—looking down at the havoc outside—cars swirling like small pieces of kelp tossed by surf—people running from that insatiably line-dancing wall of saltwater—these were not random images, like some dreams—but decade old simulacra stacked like bowls on my back shelf of memory—relics of televised helicopter footage—2011 tsunami flowing over Sukiuso, Japan—stealing our after-dinner glow—transfixing us and our hosts, Hamish and Abby in Dunedin, New Zealand, and two days ago, my eyes opened at 3:42 AM—my brain straining at how I would rescue my oldest from the dystopian universe of the Upside Down—a believable fantasy freak-show put forth by our current streaming service, and of course, there's the occasional pipe dream of involuntary infidelity with the blond coed in reverse cowgirl—when you're 60, the future is as uncertain as avocados ripening—worries legion, and true rest elusive—kids healthy? Climate change? Sea-level rise? Runaway inflation?—a full night sleep an endangered species that went extinct sometime in the last century—but sometimes I just have to pee.

International Flight

Flight 567, Atlanta-Toronto, two carry-ons, the large navy with shoulder straps guarding laptop and uke—and I wonder about the PhD defense I'm headed to—outside examiner, my official title—dissertation solid except for one major conceptual point, and the question "Why me" is burrowing through my brain folds—because this very conceptual point has been the focus of just one hundred of my published papers—and hope says "don't get sucked into some academic black hole"—an alternate conceptual universe that grabs my shirt, pulling through into several unpleasant academic hours, and because life twists us like the dough for a raw pretzel—that old chestnut, "we shall see", applies—though I'm thinking I should have read that dissertation microscopically before agreeing—but hey, free trip to Toronto—unseen for decades, the polychromatic fish stalls in Kensington Market still pop up in my memory banks from a visit decades ago, and this may be my last free work trip—travel sans costs now almost the sole perk of the professoriate, because, the "business model" has won the war—administrators no longer lifted from the ranks of esteemed scholars, but just clerks ascended to knighthood—bereft of honor—sinverguenza in Spanish—no scholarship, nor teaching, only budgets and donor seduction—pressuring even secretaries and custodians to "give back"—their salaries and benefits thin as the frothy scum at the bottom of a latte glass.

Forty years, I've been inside the belly of the whale. Two months retired—I'm struggling to learn how one lives underneath a warm custard sun.

Growing up Poor

is like *Herpes simplex*—it's
never cured, won't leave,
always wants to hang. It
just lays there silently,
until life chews me up
and spits me out, like my
first bite of cheap steak—then,
and only then, it slaloms
down a nerve to bloom—
a red peony on
my upper lip.

Years later, mortgage mostly
paid off, bank account flush as
a king tide, the gaunt fingers
of poverty still crawl the
canyon walls of my brain,
whispering "Don't. Too risky.
You won't succeed."

Reaching up, yet again,
I pry away those bony
articulations of the past.

Cause Unknown

My town is creative—music, art,
literature. Most come for college,
stay on—futoning house to house—
fiscal sustenance a carousel
with only part-time horses—barista,
server, barback, cashier, revolving
year by year—rent, food, car insurance,
gas—chances at club gigs, group shows,
open mics, art openings, and signings.

It's a granitic life—millennia
of heat and pressure—the "break"
just around the corner of Lumpkin
and Clayton—always taking a toll.

After thirty years I still cry,

every time I read an obituary
stating "cause unknown".

Clicking on the Heart

Fifteen years on Facebook—my ropes
well worked and burnished—yet I
find myself clicking the heart
emoji all day long—it's not
love welling up for every
cat post, yoga selfie, or
pumpkin pie, redolent with
clove and allspice, but in a
life of masking and quarantine,
the thumbs up seems wanting—even
its color is blue-cold—although
surveys teach, blue is everyone's
favorite shade.

It's Pandemic year three, new
strains pushing up like daffodils
in March, and the Reaper
ringing every door bell—sliding
through every unlocked window—
but I will click each heart
possible—telling the truth—
love isn't exhaustible—
not a commodity that
is devalued through stock
buy-backs—and though here in
year three I am withered like
a crushed paper bag—clicking
the heart emoji is a
contribution I can still make.

Retirement Poem Four

Cleaning Out My Office

Photographs saved for last—
family chronology in
eleven frames, gilt, maple,
and burled walnut.

No pictures of my beloved—a
gem not unveiled for colleagues—
the line between friend and work.

But my daughters, yes—my
daily dose of joy—the rose
and lily bud and bloom, as budget
cuts decapitate scholarship,
and grant money wears the crown.

The first photo—me and the
baby veterinarian, 1994—I am
forty, she is one and a half.
Summer—her frilly pink bathing
suit, compliments my white tank-top
and green running shorts.

Solo shots—three and four—
summertime again, favorite
dresses—Smokey the cat,
grasped behind his forelegs, wears
a tolerant grimace.

Number two, the neuroscientist,
arrives four years later. She is
tranquil as the first is active—
and I tumble to the fact that
behavior is a roll of genetic dice.

Decades pass—pictures echo
milestones and mundanity.
Sisters together, missing teeth
Bat Mitzvahs and graduations,
Cum Laude and Summa.

Where will these photos hang
in a new life?

Where will I place so much
unearned joy?

Sketchy Old Man

Before my lectures I
jog five miles.

Part on Milledge Avenue—
heart of town.

Sorority and frat houses,
like piano keys.

Athens, Georgia—I
greet all.

And yesterday heard
"Did you see that

sketch old man
who tried to talk to me?"

Great Blue Heron

Our rental cottage bears scars from
Hurricane Alex, five years past,
when Horsepen Creek rose over both dock
and back porch, entering the house
without key or payment, but karma-wise,
the Atlantic was just collecting its
due tithe. No matter—our vacation
homeplace for decades. First we were two,
then three and finally four.

It is early August.

In two weeks we return to the
lecture room, but now it's 6:45
AM and I'm drinking my second
cup of Sumatran Mandheling, having
walked over to the Fifth Street beach
to watch the sun summit the Atlantic
horizon, and yes, the rays do run
across the sky, just like phaser bursts
from the Enterprise, but now, on
the back deck of the house I'm watching
our local great blue heron stalk
killifish and fiddler crabs at ebb tide

Even in my seventh decade I
am not a patient man, and I wish
I could slow or halt myself, just
for ten minutes, like this bird from

a Ming dynasty scroll painting by
Shen Zhou, a monk's flowing silk robes,
contemplation of the wind, or lack of
wind, and suddenly the bird takes a
tremendous shit, all white uric acid
and crab parts, and I remember that
we are all one.

The Emotions of Trees

Who knew trees communicate—
that Douglas firs sooth white alder,
and fallen tulip poplars
nourish yellow birch seedlings
at their breasts—nurse logs their name.

Both incense cedar and madrone
have confided that all trees admire,
even envy, coastal and interior
redwoods, but avoid that needy,
millennia old, bristlecone pine, who
thinks every minute is a new day.

Once, while hiking in Oglethorpe
County, two water oaks asked me
to join their healing circle for a
distant cousin, a Black Tupelo
with terminal heart rot. So strange,
a minyan for trees is only three.

Over time, I've watched our local
black walnut shake with laughter as
English ivy first tiptoed over
its roots—only to tremble anxiously
two years later as the vine started
to choke its crown, thieving sap and light.

And the selfishness of mistletoe
leaves me speechless.

Trees demand so much intimacy,
branches straining outwards—secrets
shedding from every leaf.

Many times I hike back to the car little
more than a half-filled husk.

DeKaye's Brown Snake

It is the most common unseen snake,
sliding through the work of last year's
red oak and maple, taupe leaves now asleep
under my azaleas and Dutch irises.

DeKaye's is the shy kid in the
serpent seventh grade. The tween
bracing the green gymnasium
wall at the ophidian school dance.

Not just shy, but short, like so many
middle-schoolers—typical max. size
a foot, with occasional giants of
twenty inches—like the six-foot kid
who flunked eighth grade and was held back.

Its chitinous scales are pastel, not oil—
tan, cream, and brown, sometimes a handful
of black-spots, as if Shelley's fountain
pen mistakenly spurted on a blank
page—mottled skin disappearing
into the Piedmont duff.

Typically, I hear their rustling before sighting—
they are cryptic as a fired principal.

Eight years ago I picked up a fat female
and two-dozen young parachuted out,
only to scatter in October's leaves

like camoed members of some covert
Navy Seal action.

I'm at a loss for its love of slugs.

Bomb Cyclone in Athens, Georgia

The wind slapped me like Crazy Aunt Blossom
did when she lost it—nieces, nephews, even
adult relations scared shit-less of her, so everyone
just stood around, whistling and regarding
something else, which proves history does
repeat itself—air, my silent witness
while the wind has its way with my cheeks
and nose, both desiccated scarlet—although
a half-mile remains in my jog—thoughts
speculating on whether someone will
find me in fetal position on Springdale,
like an Incan mummy from some stratospheric
Andean cave, nothing left but shoe-leather skin,
heart, liver and lungs, which reminds me of the
effort needed to really live—pump primed every
day with taste, touch, and scent—piney candles—
warm showers reverting us to the sea
of the unborn, hand-made pasta, and Brunello,
but the temperature is now 18 Fahrenheit,
sans that show-off, Mr. Wind-Chill, and I hang
a left on Woodlawn Avenue, abandoning
this endorphin fantasy of jogging
during a Bomb Cyclone, and head for home
as my nose starts running faster than my feet.

The Day I Almost Dropped the Torah

Perhaps it was the altitude,
Salt Lake City an unrolled omelet
thirty-two hundred feet higher
than my backyard, with a March
wind that cut like a just honed filet knife
trimming up lox.

Looking east, the Wasatch Mountains
were a string of upside down sugar
cones, with vanilla ice cream
dribbling from the peaks.

Or maybe it was jet lag--my cells
unhappy with the two-hour
time subtraction from Georgia.

But yesterday, I came close to dropping a Torah.

This trip is for Cousin Jessica's
Bat Mitzvah, a rarity in my
21st century, areligious
family—now a rite of choice, not
obligation. I remain one who
practices our faith, and have the
honor of Hagbah, a reenactment
of the Prophet Ezra's unrolling
the embryonic holy Torah text
for view by the Judeans—not
rocket science, but physically taxing—
a job of love, and respect.

Each hand-scribed Torah, is wound onto
long, top-heavy, wooden spindles—thirty
pounds more or less. I am now Ezra,
unfurling the scroll until the requisite
three columns of text are viewable, then
levering it up off the bima, I
turn towards the tabernacle, lifting
the open scroll, one spindle in each
hand, high over my head, for the
congregation to see.

Suddenly, the right spindle decides that
it's Joseph in his multi-colored coat,
while the left becomes his brothers, acting
out the original jealous sin
of casting Joseph down into the
cistern, and as my control struggles to
fly away like the stained glass doves in
the sanctuary windows, I grasp
that now I'm a true Israelite
metaphorically speaking, wrestling
not with G-d, but with his words. I quickly
clench my fingers around the maple
handles, and lower the scroll with the help
of my spotter, the rabbinical intern.
Seated, clasping the scroll to my chest,
breath returning to normal—my wife begins
to dress the Torah and says, "don't worry
nobody noticed."

Boats Floating Downstream

I watch the convoy weave downstream,
past the tan-fingered roots of the old
box elder—eleven of us standing
on the slippery clay bank, brick-clay
they called it a hundred years ago,
as my thoughts begin to climb through a
sky so incisively azure it forced
October to arrive.

Our brows wrinkle, then ease—recalling
what we've written on these white paper
dinghies—"Mom, I hated that your illness
made me the parent; please forgive me". "My
son, how could I have not seen you slipping
away, I know I could have done more"

Every Rosh Hashanah we perform
Tashlich, writing down our sins—omission
and commission, crumpling them into
paper boats, then launching them on
some nearby stream.

Vessels of release—hauling our
transgressions downstream, they
grant absolution—easing our rebirth
into the new year.

The Hours of Prayer

1. **Lauds**
A nightmare wakes me—repeated theme—I can't get to Barajas, the Madrid airport—I will miss my plane—but the subtext is "go to the damn bathroom"—so I throw back the percale sheet, roll to the right, and plant my slightly wobbly, 4:32AM, feet on our red oak floor—take a right at the hall—and enter the yellow bathroom—eight seconds later I am lifting the wooden toilet seat and peeing.

2. **Prime**
Awake for an hour—sleep escaped for the night—again, I roll to my right, stand up, grab shorts, tee-shirt, flip-flops, my current novel—historical fiction about the Marranos, the crypto-Jews of 15th century Spain—walk to the living room and turn on both the floor and table lamps. It is early September and sunrise is two hours distant.

3. **Terce**
I sit on the couch while the sun shovels a seemingly inexhaustible supply of light into our living room—thirty pages read—email checked—happy birthday greetings sent to twelve Facebook friends, even checked my Insta. My coffee cup snuggles the lamp on our mahogany side table—empty after three fillings.

4. **Sext**
Nothing for lunch—not penance—but easier to lose the extra ten pounds this way—hunger chased away by a four-mile jog—mid-day is hot, already in the 90's—sweat rolls down me like a missed fast ball on a steep street.

5. **None**
It's nap time, but as usual I scare it off—two cups of strong coffee in the neighborhood coffeehouse—temptation everywhere—scones, cheese Danish, fruit tarts—but the writing goes well.

6. **Vespers**
Supper has come and gone—shrimp salad, steamed asparagus, baguette from the bakery, and Comté cheese to finish—the bones of three poems rest on the computer desktop—skin and muscles to be added on the marrow—air, sweet with satisfaction.

7. **Night Watch**
A nightmare wakes me…

Cumulus Clouds, Clarke County, Georgia

Two PM on July tenth—the sun
broils every outbreath, but this cosseted
afternoon, the sky is strewn with
cumulus clouds, neither altocumulus,
nor stratocumulus, just plain old
cumulus dumplings pushing through the
Tropospheric broth. Climatologists
call them—"well developed", and these were
meticulously placed by Odin or Yahweh,
because only a g-d could distribute
these clouds so evenly—like the white
squares on a new chess board, or the
Spanish Armada—sails full, and tacking
up the French coast. This is not some
random tableau, but cobalt sky
and cotton boll clouds painted by
Van Gogh on a morn when he knew fact
from fancy, but still they puzzle—each
separate, yet linked, like a chain fence—all
intention and purpose. They must
represent something and I scratch my head
in query—are they failing marriages,
fully charged and about to bolt? Are
they residual lacy valentines
from Miss Schaefer's fifth grade class—I pined
for one from Cathy Smith? Or are they
just my brain's demand for order
and purpose in this anxious and
chaotic world?

The Weight of the World

1. This poem is not about the Russian invasion of Ukraine.

2. This poem is not about starving children in Congo.

3. This poem is not about global warming.

4. This poem is not about immigrant children in jail.

5. This poem is not about shortages of potable water.

6.This poem is not about clearcutting the Amazon
rainforest.
7. This poem is not about racism.

8. This poem is about peeling back the borders of my heart—
of grasping, that doing something, anything—often is
just enough.

9. It's about eating both peanut butter cups in the package
of life, because two is a prime number
and therefore perfect.

10. In 2 CE Talmudic scholars wrote: "Do not be daunted by
the enormity of the world's grief. Do justly now. Love
mercy now. Walk humbly now. It is not your duty to
complete the task, nor are you free to abandon it."

11. Every day I push back my boundaries—reminding
myself that both Renoir and Cezanne painted by
stitching together small squares of colored light.

The Celadon Vase

You always loved the color
celadon—jade, hoisted from earth—
to clothe stiff-necked porcelain—from
an East so distant that small migrating
birds travel West to arrive.

After you left, the front door
wouldn't close, and I wondered
if you were the storm-wind—seeking
a way back inside.

Spirits are persistent, and need no
timepiece.

Your vases still sit upon our
maple dresser.

The Rhythms of Various Bodies

Celestial globes rise and set—
our bodies stepping to the daily
waltz of sun and moon. Circadian,
the twenty-four-hour rhythm—moving
on to daily, monthly, annual,
cycles.

Neither tree nor fish, our yearly growth
rings are unseen—first cycle felt is
monthly, uterine lining waxing
and waning, painting the moon carmine
with tears, or joy, as pulse, blood tension,
and body warmth, dance with light and dark—
sleep and waking.

We begin helpless—then learning—
then doing—sliding back to
feebleness—then quiet—finally,
the last
breath.

About the Author

Gary Grossman is Professor Emeritus of Animal Ecology at University of Georgia, and an author of 150 scientific articles, Gary's poetry has been published in 40+ reviews including: Verse-Virtual, Sheila-Na-Gig, MacQueen's Quinterly, Salvation South, and Delta Poetry Review. Short fiction in MacQueen's and creative non-fiction in Tamarind Literary Magazine. Gary's flash fiction piece "Mindfulness" was nominated by MacQueen's Quinterly for inclusion in The Best Small Fictions 2023. For 10 years he wrote the "Ask Dr. Trout" column for American Angler Magazine. Gary's first poetry book Lyrical Years is available from Kelsay Press and Amazon, and his graphic novel My Life in Fish: One Scientist's Journey, also available from Impspired, may be purchased on Amazon. His gourmet venison cookbook A Bone to Pick. My Life in Fish… may be purchased from Amazon or todaysecologicalsolutions@gmail.com . Website: https://www.garygrossman.net/ , Blog: https://medium.com/@garydavidgrossman .